Shrimp Sensations

A Pasta Lover's Guide to Delectable Seafood Delights

While every precaution has been taken in the preparation of this book, the publisher assumes no responsibility for errors or omissions, or for damages resulting from the use of the information contained herein.

SHRIMP SENSATIONS

First edition. February 11, 2024.

Copyright © 2024 Jose Maria.

ISBN: 979-8224013418

Written by Jose Maria.

Table of Contents

Jose Maria

❖ Introduction

A. Welcome to the World of Shrimp Pasta

Welcome, pasta lovers, to a culinary journey filled with the irresistible flavors of shrimp and pasta! In this guide, we'll explore the delightful fusion of succulent shrimp and al dente pasta, creating dishes that tantalize the taste buds and satisfy the soul. Whether you're a seasoned chef or a novice in the kitchen, get ready to immerse yourself in the world of Shrimp Sensations.

B. Brief History of Shrimp Pasta

The marriage of shrimp and pasta traces its roots back to ancient culinary traditions. In coastal regions around the world, where both seafood and pasta were abundant, locals began combining these ingredients to create flavorful and hearty dishes. Over time, shrimp pasta recipes evolved, influenced by various cultures and culinary techniques.

Today, shrimp pasta has become a beloved staple in cuisines worldwide, from classic Italian dishes like Shrimp Scampi to exotic Thai-inspired creations. Its versatility and deliciousness continue to captivate food enthusiasts of all backgrounds, making it a timeless favorite on dinner tables everywhere.

C. Tips for Cooking Perfect Shrimp Pasta Every Time

Mastering the art of shrimp pasta requires attention to detail and a few essential tips to ensure culinary success:

1. Choose Quality Ingredients: Start with fresh, high-quality shrimp and premium pasta for the best results. Opt for sustainable seafood options whenever possible.
2. Proper Shrimp Preparation: Whether you're using fresh or frozen shrimp, be sure to devein and remove the shells before cooking. This enhances the presentation and texture of the dish.
3. Don't Overcook the Shrimp: Shrimp cook quickly and can become tough and rubbery if overcooked. Cook them just until

they turn pink and opaque, usually within 2-3 minutes per side.

4. Season Thoughtfully: Enhance the flavor of your shrimp pasta with a balanced combination of herbs, spices, and aromatics. Garlic, lemon, parsley, and red pepper flakes are classic choices that complement the natural sweetness of shrimp.

5. Perfect Pasta Preparation: Cook pasta until it's al dente, meaning it's firm to the bite. This ensures the pasta maintains its texture and doesn't become mushy when combined with the shrimp and sauce.

With these tips in mind, you're ready to embark on a delicious culinary adventure with shrimp pasta. Let's dive into the recipes and discover the myriad ways to enjoy this delectable combination!

Chapter (1) Getting Started with Shrimp and Pasta

A. Choosing the Right Shrimp

Selecting the perfect shrimp is essential for creating delicious shrimp pasta dishes. Here are some tips to help you choose the right shrimp:

1. Freshness: Look for shrimp that have a mild, ocean-like scent. Avoid shrimp with a strong fishy odor, as it may indicate that the shrimp is not fresh.
2. Appearance: Choose shrimp that are firm, translucent, and shiny. Avoid shrimp that appear dull, discolored, or slimy.
3. Size: Shrimp are typically categorized by size, ranging from extra-small to jumbo. Consider the recipe you're preparing and choose the appropriate size shrimp accordingly. Larger shrimp are ideal for grilling or sautéing, while smaller shrimp work well in pasta dishes.
4. Shell-on vs. Peeled: Decide whether you want to use shrimp with the shell on or peeled. Shell-on shrimp tend to have more flavor but require additional preparation, such as deveining and removing the shell. Peeled shrimp are convenient and ready to use but may lack some flavor.
5. Sustainability: Whenever possible, choose sustainably sourced shrimp to support responsible fishing practices and minimize environmental impact.

By carefully selecting fresh, high-quality shrimp, you'll enhance the flavor and overall enjoyment of your shrimp pasta dishes.

B. Selecting the Perfect Pasta

Choosing the right pasta is equally important for creating the perfect shrimp pasta dish. Consider the following factors when selecting pasta:

1. Shape: Different pasta shapes pair better with certain sauces and ingredients. Long, thin pasta like linguine or spaghetti is ideal for lighter sauces, while short pasta shapes like penne or fusilli are better suited for thicker sauces and hearty ingredients.

2. Texture: Pay attention to the texture of the pasta. Al dente pasta, cooked until it's firm to the bite, is preferred for most pasta dishes. It ensures that the pasta holds its shape and absorbs the sauce properly.

3. Flavor: Some pasta varieties are flavored with ingredients like spinach, tomato, or squid ink, adding an extra dimension of flavor to your dish. Consider experimenting with different flavored pastas to enhance the overall taste of your shrimp pasta.

4. Fresh vs. Dried: While fresh pasta has a shorter cooking time and a softer texture, dried pasta is more convenient and has a longer shelf life. Choose the type of pasta based on your preferences and the specific requirements of your recipe.

5. Gluten-Free Options: If you or your guests have dietary restrictions, consider using gluten-free pasta made from alternative flours like rice, quinoa, or chickpea flour.

By selecting the perfect pasta for your shrimp pasta recipe, you'll ensure a harmonious combination of flavors and textures.

C. Essential Ingredients and Kitchen Tools

Before you begin cooking shrimp pasta, gather the essential ingredients and kitchen tools you'll need:

Ingredients:

- Fresh or frozen shrimp
- Pasta of your choice
- Olive oil or butter

- Garlic
- Lemon
- Fresh herbs (such as parsley or basil)
- Red pepper flakes (optional)
- Salt and pepper
- Parmesan cheese (for garnish)

Kitchen Tools:

- Large pot for boiling pasta
- Skillet or sauté pan for cooking shrimp and sauce
- Colander for draining cooked pasta
- Sharp knife and cutting board for chopping ingredients
- Garlic press or microplane for mincing garlic
- Lemon juicer
- Tongs or spatula for tossing pasta and shrimp
- Grater for grating Parmesan cheese

Having these ingredients and tools on hand will make the cooking process smooth and enjoyable, allowing you to focus on creating delicious shrimp pasta dishes. Now that you're equipped with the knowledge and resources to get started, let's dive into the recipes and bring your shrimp pasta creations to life!

Chapter (2) Classic Shrimp Pasta Recipes

A. Shrimp Scampi Linguine

Ingredients:

- 1 pound linguine pasta
- 1 pound large shrimp, peeled and deveined
- 4 cloves garlic, minced
- 1/4 cup olive oil
- 1/4 cup dry white wine
- 1/4 cup freshly squeezed lemon juice
- Zest of 1 lemon
- 1/4 teaspoon red pepper flakes (optional)
- Salt and pepper to taste
- 1/4 cup chopped fresh parsley
- Grated Parmesan cheese for serving

Instructions:

1. Cook linguine pasta according to package instructions until al dente. Drain and set aside, reserving 1/2 cup of pasta water.
2. In a large skillet, heat olive oil over medium heat. Add minced garlic and cook until fragrant, about 1 minute.
3. Add the shrimp to the skillet and season with salt, pepper, and red pepper flakes (if using). Cook shrimp until pink and opaque, about 2-3 minutes per side.
4. Deglaze the skillet with white wine, scraping up any browned bits from the bottom. Allow the wine to reduce by half.
5. Add lemon juice and lemon zest to the skillet, stirring to combine. Cook for another minute.
6. Toss the cooked linguine pasta with the shrimp and sauce in the skillet. If the sauce is too thick, add some of the reserved pasta

water to loosen it.

7. Sprinkle chopped parsley over the shrimp scampi linguine and toss to incorporate.

8. Serve hot, garnished with grated Parmesan cheese. Enjoy this classic shrimp pasta dish with a squeeze of fresh lemon juice!

9. Stay tuned for the next classic shrimp pasta recipe: Creamy Garlic Shrimp Fettuccine Alfredo.

B. Creamy Garlic Shrimp Fettuccine Alfredo
Ingredients:

- 1 pound fettuccine pasta
- 1 pound large shrimp, peeled and deveined
- 4 cloves garlic, minced
- 1/4 cup unsalted butter
- 1 cup heavy cream
- 1 cup freshly grated Parmesan cheese
- Salt and pepper to taste
- 1/4 teaspoon nutmeg (optional)
- Chopped fresh parsley for garnish

Instructions:

1. Cook fettuccine pasta according to package instructions until al dente. Drain and set aside.

2. In a large skillet, melt the butter over medium heat. Add minced garlic and cook until fragrant, about 1 minute.

3. Add the shrimp to the skillet and season with salt and pepper. Cook shrimp until pink and opaque, about 2-3 minutes per side. Remove shrimp from the skillet and set aside.

4. In the same skillet, pour in the heavy cream and bring to a simmer. Allow the cream to reduce slightly, stirring occasionally, for about 5 minutes.

5. Gradually add the grated Parmesan cheese to the skillet, stirring constantly until the cheese is melted and the sauce is smooth and creamy.
6. If desired, season the sauce with nutmeg for an extra layer of flavor.
7. Return the cooked shrimp to the skillet and toss to coat them in the creamy Alfredo sauce.
8. Add the cooked fettuccine pasta to the skillet and toss until evenly coated in the sauce.
9. Serve hot, garnished with chopped fresh parsley and additional grated Parmesan cheese if desired. Enjoy this indulgent and comforting creamy garlic shrimp fettuccine Alfredo!

Stay tuned for the next classic shrimp pasta recipe: Spicy Shrimp Arrabbiata Penne.

C. Spicy Shrimp Arrabbiata Penne
Ingredients:

- 1 pound penne pasta
- 1 pound large shrimp, peeled and deveined
- 4 cloves garlic, minced
- 2 tablespoons olive oil
- 1 can (14 ounces) crushed tomatoes
- 1/4 teaspoon red pepper flakes (adjust to taste)
- 1 teaspoon dried oregano
- Salt and pepper to taste
- Chopped fresh basil for garnish
- Grated Parmesan cheese for serving

Instructions:

1. Cook penne pasta according to package instructions until al dente. Drain and set aside.

2. In a large skillet, heat olive oil over medium heat. Add minced garlic and red pepper flakes, and cook until fragrant, about 1 minute.
3. Add the shrimp to the skillet and season with salt, pepper, and dried oregano. Cook shrimp until pink and opaque, about 2-3 minutes per side. Remove shrimp from the skillet and set aside.
4. In the same skillet, pour in the crushed tomatoes and bring to a simmer. Allow the sauce to cook for about 10 minutes, stirring occasionally, until slightly thickened.
5. Return the cooked shrimp to the skillet and toss to coat them in the spicy Arrabbiata sauce.
6. Add the cooked penne pasta to the skillet and toss until evenly coated in the sauce.
7. Serve hot, garnished with chopped fresh basil and grated Parmesan cheese. Enjoy this flavorful and spicy shrimp Arrabbiata penne pasta!

Stay tuned for the final classic shrimp pasta recipe: Lemon Garlic Shrimp Orzo.

D. Lemon Garlic Shrimp Orzo
  Ingredients:

- 1 cup orzo pasta
- 1 pound large shrimp, peeled and deveined
- 4 cloves garlic, minced
- Zest of 1 lemon
- Juice of 1 lemon
- 2 tablespoons olive oil
- 2 tablespoons unsalted butter
- Salt and pepper to taste
- Chopped fresh parsley for garnish

- Grated Parmesan cheese for serving

Instructions:

1. Cook orzo pasta according to package instructions until al dente. Drain and set aside.
2. In a large skillet, heat olive oil and butter over medium heat. Add minced garlic and cook until fragrant, about 1 minute.
3. Add the shrimp to the skillet and season with salt and pepper. Cook shrimp until pink and opaque, about 2-3 minutes per side.
4. Once the shrimp are cooked, remove them from the skillet and set aside.
5. In the same skillet, add the cooked orzo pasta, lemon zest, and lemon juice. Toss to combine and heat through.
6. Return the cooked shrimp to the skillet and toss with the orzo until evenly coated.
7. Season with additional salt and pepper if needed.
8. Serve hot, garnished with chopped fresh parsley and grated Parmesan cheese. Enjoy this light and flavorful lemon garlic shrimp orzo dish!

With these classic shrimp pasta recipes, you'll be well on your way to mastering the art of creating delicious seafood delights. If you have any questions or need further assistance, feel free to ask. Bon appétit!

Chapter (3) Creative Shrimp Pasta Variations

A. Shrimp and Spinach Stuffed Shells
Ingredients:

- 12 large pasta shells
- 1 pound large shrimp, peeled and deveined
- 2 cups fresh spinach, chopped
- 1 cup ricotta cheese
- 1/2 cup shredded mozzarella cheese
- 1/4 cup grated Parmesan cheese
- 2 cloves garlic, minced
- 1 tablespoon olive oil
- Salt and pepper to taste
- Marinara sauce for serving

Instructions:

1. Cook pasta shells according to package instructions until al dente. Drain and set aside.
2. In a large skillet, heat olive oil over medium heat. Add minced garlic and cook until fragrant, about 1 minute.
3. Add shrimp to the skillet and cook until pink and opaque, about 2-3 minutes per side. Remove shrimp from the skillet, chop into small pieces, and set aside.
4. In a mixing bowl, combine chopped shrimp, chopped spinach, ricotta cheese, mozzarella cheese, Parmesan cheese, salt, and pepper.
5. Preheat oven to 375°F (190°C).
6. Stuff each cooked pasta shell with the shrimp and spinach mixture.

7. Spread a thin layer of marinara sauce on the bottom of a baking dish. Place stuffed shells in the dish.

8. Cover the dish with aluminum foil and bake for 20-25 minutes, or until heated through.

9. Serve hot, garnished with additional grated Parmesan cheese if desired.

B. Cajun Shrimp and Sausage Pasta
Ingredients:

- 1 pound penne pasta
- 1 pound large shrimp, peeled and deveined
- 1/2 pound smoked sausage, sliced
- 1 bell pepper, diced
- 1 onion, diced
- 2 cloves garlic, minced
- 1 tablespoon Cajun seasoning
- 1 cup heavy cream
- 1/2 cup chicken broth
- 2 tablespoons olive oil
- Salt and pepper to taste
- Chopped fresh parsley for garnish

Instructions:

1. Cook penne pasta according to package instructions until al dente. Drain and set aside.

2. In a large skillet, heat olive oil over medium heat. Add diced onion, bell pepper, and minced garlic. Cook until softened, about 5 minutes.

3. Add sliced sausage to the skillet and cook until lightly browned.

4. Season shrimp with Cajun seasoning. Add seasoned shrimp to the skillet and cook until pink and opaque, about 2-3 minutes

per side.

5. Pour in heavy cream and chicken broth, stirring to combine. Allow the sauce to simmer for about 5 minutes, until slightly thickened.
6. Add cooked penne pasta to the skillet and toss to coat in the Cajun sauce.
7. Season with salt and pepper to taste.
8. Serve hot, garnished with chopped fresh parsley.

Stay tuned for the next creative shrimp pasta variation: Shrimp and Mushroom Risotto.

C. Shrimp and Mushroom Risotto
Ingredients:

- 1 pound large shrimp, peeled and deveined
- 1 cup Arborio rice
- 4 cups chicken or vegetable broth
- 1 cup mushrooms, sliced (such as cremini or button mushrooms)
- 1 onion, finely chopped
- 2 cloves garlic, minced
- 1/2 cup dry white wine
- 1/4 cup grated Parmesan cheese
- 2 tablespoons butter
- 2 tablespoons olive oil
- Salt and pepper to taste
- Chopped fresh parsley for garnish

Instructions:

1. In a large skillet or saucepan, heat olive oil over medium heat. Add chopped onion and cook until translucent, about 5

minutes.

2. Add minced garlic and sliced mushrooms to the skillet. Cook until the mushrooms are tender and browned, about 8-10 minutes.

3. Meanwhile, in a separate saucepan, heat the chicken or vegetable broth over low heat until warm.

4. Once the mushrooms are cooked, add Arborio rice to the skillet. Stir to coat the rice with the oil and cook for 1-2 minutes until slightly toasted.

5. Pour in the white wine and cook until it is absorbed by the rice, stirring constantly.

6. Begin adding the warm broth to the skillet, one ladleful at a time, stirring constantly and allowing each addition of broth to be absorbed before adding more. Continue this process for about 20-25 minutes, or until the rice is creamy and cooked to your desired consistency.

7. While the risotto is cooking, season the shrimp with salt and pepper. In a separate skillet, heat olive oil over medium heat. Add the seasoned shrimp and cook until pink and opaque, about 2-3 minutes per side. Remove from heat and set aside.

8. Once the risotto is cooked, stir in grated Parmesan cheese and butter until melted and creamy. Adjust seasoning with salt and pepper if needed.

9. Serve the risotto hot, topped with cooked shrimp and garnished with chopped fresh parsley.

Enjoy this luxurious and flavorful shrimp and mushroom risotto as a comforting and satisfying meal!

D. Shrimp and Pesto Farfalle

Ingredients:

- 1 pound farfalle (bowtie) pasta
- 1 pound large shrimp, peeled and deveined

- 1 cup basil pesto (homemade or store-bought)
- 1/4 cup pine nuts, toasted (optional)
- 2 tablespoons olive oil
- 2 cloves garlic, minced
- Salt and pepper to taste
- Grated Parmesan cheese for serving
- Fresh basil leaves for garnish

Instructions:

1. Cook farfalle pasta according to package instructions until al dente. Drain and set aside, reserving 1/2 cup of pasta water.
2. In a large skillet, heat olive oil over medium heat. Add minced garlic and cook until fragrant, about 1 minute.
3. Add the shrimp to the skillet and season with salt and pepper. Cook shrimp until pink and opaque, about 2-3 minutes per side. Remove shrimp from the skillet and set aside.
4. In the same skillet, add the cooked farfalle pasta and pesto sauce. Toss to coat the pasta evenly in the pesto, adding reserved pasta water as needed to loosen the sauce.
5. Return the cooked shrimp to the skillet and toss with the pesto-coated farfalle until well combined.
6. Toast pine nuts in a dry skillet over medium heat for 2-3 minutes until lightly browned and fragrant. Be careful not to burn them.
7. Serve hot, garnished with toasted pine nuts, grated Parmesan cheese, and fresh basil leaves.

Enjoy this vibrant and flavorful shrimp and pesto farfalle pasta, perfect for a quick and delicious weeknight dinner!

Chapter (4) International Shrimp Pasta Delights

A. Thai Shrimp Pad Thai
Ingredients:

- 8 ounces rice noodles
- 1/2 pound large shrimp, peeled and deveined
- 2 eggs, lightly beaten
- 2 cloves garlic, minced
- 2 tablespoons tamarind paste
- 2 tablespoons fish sauce
- 1 tablespoon soy sauce
- 1 tablespoon brown sugar
- 1 tablespoon vegetable oil
- 1 cup bean sprouts
- 1/2 cup chopped green onions
- 1/4 cup chopped peanuts
- Lime wedges for serving
- Fresh cilantro for garnish

Instructions:

1. Cook rice noodles according to package instructions until tender. Drain and set aside.
2. In a small bowl, whisk together tamarind paste, fish sauce, soy sauce, and brown sugar to make the sauce. Set aside.
3. Heat vegetable oil in a large skillet or wok over medium-high heat. Add minced garlic and cook for 30 seconds.
4. Add shrimp to the skillet and cook until pink and opaque, about 2-3 minutes. Push the shrimp to one side of the skillet and add beaten eggs to the other side. Scramble the eggs until

cooked through.

5. Add cooked rice noodles to the skillet along with the prepared sauce. Toss everything together until well combined.
6. Add bean sprouts and chopped green onions to the skillet, tossing to combine with the noodles and shrimp.
7. Serve hot, garnished with chopped peanuts, lime wedges, and fresh cilantro.

B. Spanish Shrimp Paella Pasta
Ingredients:

- 8 ounces spaghetti or linguine pasta
- 1/2 pound large shrimp, peeled and deveined
- 1/2 cup chorizo sausage, sliced
- 1 onion, diced
- 2 cloves garlic, minced
- 1 red bell pepper, diced
- 1 cup diced tomatoes (fresh or canned)
- 1 teaspoon smoked paprika
- 1/2 teaspoon saffron threads (optional)
- 2 cups chicken broth
- Salt and pepper to taste
- Fresh parsley for garnish
- Lemon wedges for serving

Instructions:

1. Cook pasta according to package instructions until al dente. Drain and set aside.
2. In a large skillet or paella pan, heat olive oil over medium heat. Add sliced chorizo sausage and cook until browned, about 3-4 minutes.
3. Add diced onion, minced garlic, and diced red bell pepper to

the skillet. Cook until vegetables are softened, about 5 minutes.

4. Add diced tomatoes, smoked paprika, and saffron threads (if using) to the skillet. Cook for another 2 minutes.

5. Stir in chicken broth and bring to a simmer. Add shrimp to the skillet and cook until pink and opaque, about 2-3 minutes.

6. Add cooked pasta to the skillet and toss everything together until well combined.

7. Season with salt and pepper to taste. Serve hot, garnished with fresh parsley and lemon wedges.

C. Shrimp and Broccoli Lo Mein

Ingredients:

- 8 ounces lo mein noodles or spaghetti
- 1/2 pound large shrimp, peeled and deveined
- 2 cups broccoli florets
- 2 cloves garlic, minced
- 2 tablespoons soy sauce
- 1 tablespoon oyster sauce
- 1 tablespoon hoisin sauce
- 1 teaspoon sesame oil
- 2 tablespoons vegetable oil
- Salt and pepper to taste
- Chopped green onions for garnish
- Toasted sesame seeds for garnish

Instructions:

1. Cook lo mein noodles according to package instructions until al dente. Drain and set aside.

2. In a large skillet or wok, heat vegetable oil over medium-high heat. Add minced garlic and cook for 30 seconds.

3. Add shrimp to the skillet and cook until pink and opaque, about 2-3 minutes. Remove shrimp from the skillet and set aside.
4. In the same skillet, add broccoli florets and stir-fry until tender-crisp, about 3-4 minutes.
5. In a small bowl, whisk together soy sauce, oyster sauce, hoisin sauce, and sesame oil.
6. Add cooked lo mein noodles and prepared sauce to the skillet. Toss everything together until well combined.
7. Return cooked shrimp to the skillet and toss with the noodles and broccoli until heated through.
8. Season with salt and pepper to taste. Serve hot, garnished with chopped green onions and toasted sesame seeds.

D. Italian Shrimp Scampi with Capellini
Ingredients:

- 8 ounces capellini (angel hair) pasta
- 1/2 pound large shrimp, peeled and deveined
- 4 cloves garlic, minced
- 1/4 cup white wine
- 1/4 cup chicken broth
- 2 tablespoons lemon juice
- Zest of 1 lemon
- 2 tablespoons unsalted butter
- 2 tablespoons olive oil
- Salt and pepper to taste
- Chopped fresh parsley for garnish
- Grated Parmesan cheese for serving

Instructions:

1. Cook capellini pasta according to package instructions until al

dente. Drain and set aside.

2. In a large skillet, heat olive oil over medium heat. Add minced garlic and cook until fragrant, about 1 minute.
3. Add shrimp to the skillet and season with salt and pepper. Cook shrimp until pink and opaque, about 2-3 minutes per side. Remove shrimp from the skillet and set aside.
4. Deglaze the skillet with white wine, scraping up any browned bits from the bottom. Allow the wine to reduce by half.
5. Add chicken broth, lemon juice, and lemon zest to the skillet. Bring to a simmer and cook for another 2 minutes.
6. Stir in unsalted butter until melted and sauce is smooth.
7. Return cooked capellini pasta to the skillet and toss with the sauce until well coated.
8. Return cooked shrimp to the skillet and toss with the pasta until heated through.
9. Serve hot, garnished with chopped fresh parsley and grated Parmesan cheese.

Enjoy these international shrimp pasta delights inspired by flavors from around the world!

Chapter (5) Vegetarian Options with Shrimp Alternatives

A. Vegan Shrimp Pasta Primavera
Ingredients:

- 8 ounces linguine pasta (or pasta of your choice)
- 1 package of vegan shrimp alternative (such as plant-based shrimp)
- 2 cups mixed vegetables (such as bell peppers, broccoli, carrots, and cherry tomatoes), sliced
- 2 cloves garlic, minced
- 1/4 cup olive oil
- 1/4 cup vegetable broth
- 2 tablespoons nutritional yeast
- 1 tablespoon lemon juice
- Salt and pepper to taste
- Fresh basil or parsley for garnish

Instructions:

1. Cook linguine pasta according to package instructions until al dente. Drain and set aside.
2. In a large skillet, heat olive oil over medium heat. Add minced garlic and sauté until fragrant, about 1 minute.
3. Add mixed vegetables to the skillet and cook until tender-crisp, about 5-7 minutes.
4. Meanwhile, prepare the vegan shrimp alternative according to package instructions.
5. Add cooked linguine pasta to the skillet with the vegetables.
6. Stir in vegetable broth, nutritional yeast, and lemon juice. Cook for an additional 2-3 minutes, allowing the flavors to combine.

7. Add the prepared vegan shrimp to the skillet and toss everything together until heated through.
8. Season with salt and pepper to taste.
9. Serve hot, garnished with fresh basil or parsley.

B. Tofu "Shrimp" and Vegetable Stir-Fry Noodles
Ingredients:

- 8 ounces stir-fry noodles (such as rice noodles or udon noodles)
- 1 package of tofu "shrimp" (or tofu cut into small pieces)
- 2 cups mixed vegetables (such as bell peppers, snap peas, carrots, and broccoli), sliced
- 2 cloves garlic, minced
- 2 tablespoons soy sauce
- 1 tablespoon hoisin sauce
- 1 tablespoon sesame oil
- 1 tablespoon vegetable oil
- Salt and pepper to taste
- Toasted sesame seeds for garnish
- Sliced green onions for garnish

Instructions:

1. Cook stir-fry noodles according to package instructions until al dente. Drain and set aside.
2. In a large skillet or wok, heat vegetable oil over medium-high heat. Add minced garlic and sauté until fragrant, about 1 minute.
3. Add mixed vegetables to the skillet and stir-fry until tender-crisp, about 5-7 minutes.
4. Meanwhile, prepare the tofu "shrimp" according to package instructions or cut tofu into small pieces.
5. Add cooked stir-fry noodles to the skillet with the vegetables.

6. Stir in soy sauce, hoisin sauce, and sesame oil. Cook for an additional 2-3 minutes, allowing the flavors to combine.
7. Add the prepared tofu "shrimp" to the skillet and toss everything together until heated through.
8. Season with salt and pepper to taste.
9. Serve hot, garnished with toasted sesame seeds and sliced green onions.

C. Mushroom and Asparagus Shrimp-Free Linguine
Ingredients:

- 8 ounces linguine pasta (or pasta of your choice)
- 2 cups mushrooms, sliced (such as cremini or button mushrooms)
- 1 bunch asparagus, trimmed and cut into bite-sized pieces
- 2 cloves garlic, minced
- 1/4 cup olive oil
- 1/4 cup vegetable broth
- 2 tablespoons lemon juice
- Zest of 1 lemon
- Salt and pepper to taste
- Fresh parsley for garnish
- Grated Parmesan cheese (optional)

Instructions:

1. Cook linguine pasta according to package instructions until al dente. Drain and set aside.
2. In a large skillet, heat olive oil over medium heat. Add minced garlic and sauté until fragrant, about 1 minute.
3. Add sliced mushrooms to the skillet and cook until browned and tender, about 5-7 minutes.
4. Add asparagus pieces to the skillet and cook until crisp-tender,

about 3-4 minutes.

5. Stir in vegetable broth, lemon juice, and lemon zest. Cook for an additional 2-3 minutes, allowing the flavors to combine.
6. Add cooked linguine pasta to the skillet and toss everything together until well combined.
7. Season with salt and pepper to taste.
8. Serve hot, garnished with fresh parsley and grated Parmesan cheese if desired.

Enjoy these delicious and satisfying vegetarian options with shrimp alternatives, perfect for those looking to enjoy a plant-based twist on classic shrimp pasta dishes!

Chapter (6) Side Dishes and Accompaniments

A. Garlic Bread
Ingredients:

- 1 loaf of French bread or Italian bread
- 1/2 cup unsalted butter, softened
- 4 cloves garlic, minced
- 2 tablespoons chopped fresh parsley
- Salt to taste

Instructions:

1. Preheat oven to 375°F (190°C).
2. In a small bowl, mix together softened butter, minced garlic, chopped parsley, and salt until well combined.
3. Slice the loaf of bread horizontally, but do not cut all the way through. Spread the garlic butter mixture generously between the slices.
4. Wrap the bread loaf in aluminum foil and place it on a baking sheet.
5. Bake in the preheated oven for 10-15 minutes, or until the bread is heated through and the edges are slightly crispy.
6. Serve hot, sliced into individual portions.

B. Caesar Salad
Ingredients:

- 1 head romaine lettuce, washed and chopped
- 1/2 cup Caesar salad dressing (homemade or store-bought)
- 1/4 cup grated Parmesan cheese
- 1 cup croutons

Instructions:

1. In a large salad bowl, combine chopped romaine lettuce and Caesar salad dressing. Toss until the lettuce is evenly coated.
2. Sprinkle grated Parmesan cheese over the salad.
3. Add croutons to the salad just before serving to maintain their crunch.
4. Serve chilled as a refreshing side dish.

C. Grilled Vegetables
Ingredients:

- Assorted vegetables (such as bell peppers, zucchini, eggplant, mushrooms, and cherry tomatoes), sliced or halved
- Olive oil
- Salt and pepper to taste
- Fresh herbs (such as thyme or rosemary), chopped (optional)

Instructions:

1. Preheat grill to medium-high heat.
2. Toss sliced vegetables with olive oil, salt, pepper, and fresh herbs (if using) in a large bowl until well coated.
3. Place vegetables on the preheated grill and cook for 4-5 minutes per side, or until they are tender and slightly charred.
4. Remove vegetables from the grill and transfer to a serving platter.
5. Serve hot as a flavorful and colorful side dish.

D. Breadsticks
Ingredients:

- 1 pound pizza dough, homemade or store-bought
- 1/4 cup unsalted butter, melted

- 2 cloves garlic, minced
- 1/4 cup grated Parmesan cheese
- 1 tablespoon chopped fresh parsley
- Salt to taste

Instructions:

1. Preheat oven to 400°F (200°C). Line a baking sheet with parchment paper.
2. Roll out the pizza dough on a lightly floured surface into a rectangle, about 1/4 inch thick.
3. Cut the dough into strips, about 1 inch wide.
4. Twist each strip of dough and place it on the prepared baking sheet.
5. In a small bowl, mix together melted butter, minced garlic, grated Parmesan cheese, chopped parsley, and salt.
6. Brush the garlic butter mixture over the breadsticks, coating them evenly.
7. Bake in the preheated oven for 12-15 minutes, or until the breadsticks are golden brown and crispy.
8. Serve hot, accompanied by your favorite dipping sauce, such as marinara sauce or garlic aioli.

Enjoy these delicious side dishes and accompaniments alongside your shrimp pasta creations for a complete and satisfying meal!

Chapter (7) Tips for Perfecting Your Shrimp Pasta

A. Cooking Techniques for Shrimp:

1. Properly Clean and Devein: Before cooking shrimp, ensure they are properly cleaned and deveined to remove any grit or impurities.
2. Avoid Overcooking: Shrimp cook quickly, usually within 2-3 minutes per side. Be cautious not to overcook them, as they can become rubbery and lose their delicate flavor.
3. Season Well: Shrimp benefit from simple seasoning such as salt, pepper, and a squeeze of lemon juice. Don't overpower them with too many spices.
4. Grilling or Sauteing: Shrimp can be grilled or sautéed for a quick and flavorful cooking method. Use high heat and a minimal amount of oil to achieve a nicely caramelized exterior.
5. Adding to Pasta: If adding shrimp to pasta dishes, cook them separately from the pasta and add them at the end to prevent overcooking.

B. Proper Pasta Cooking Methods:

1. Use Ample Water: When cooking pasta, use a large pot with plenty of water to prevent sticking and ensure even cooking.
2. Salt the Water: Add salt to the boiling water before adding the pasta to enhance its flavor.
3. Al Dente Texture: Cook pasta until al dente, meaning it is cooked through but still slightly firm to the bite. Test the pasta a couple of minutes before the suggested cooking time on the package.
4. Reserve Pasta Water: Before draining the cooked pasta, reserve

some of the pasta water. This starchy water can be used to thin sauces and help them adhere better to the pasta.

C. Flavor Pairing Suggestions:

1. Garlic and Lemon: The classic combination of garlic and lemon complements the natural sweetness of shrimp perfectly.
2. Creamy Sauces: Creamy sauces like Alfredo or carbonara pair well with shrimp, adding richness and depth to the dish.
3. Spicy Flavors: Shrimp can handle spicy flavors well. Consider adding red pepper flakes, chili powder, or hot sauce for a kick.
4. Herbs: Fresh herbs such as parsley, basil, and cilantro add brightness and freshness to shrimp pasta dishes.
5. Citrus Zest: Incorporating citrus zest, such as lemon or lime, adds a burst of flavor and freshness to shrimp pasta.

D. Serving and Presentation Tips:

1. Garnish: Sprinkle chopped fresh herbs, grated Parmesan cheese, or toasted nuts over the finished dish for added flavor and visual appeal.
2. Plating: Use wide-rimmed bowls or plates for serving shrimp pasta, allowing for easy mixing and enjoyment.
3. Individual Servings: Consider portioning the shrimp pasta into individual servings for a polished presentation.
4. Accompaniments: Serve shrimp pasta with complementary side dishes such as garlic bread, Caesar salad, or grilled vegetables to round out the meal.
5. Freshness: Serve shrimp pasta immediately after cooking to ensure the shrimp are tender and the pasta is al dente.

By following these tips, you can elevate your shrimp pasta dishes to a new level of perfection, creating flavorful and satisfying meals every time.

Chapter (8) Desserts to Complete the Meal

A. Tiramisu

Ingredients:

- 6 egg yolks
- 3/4 cup granulated sugar
- 1 cup mascarpone cheese
- 1 1/2 cups heavy cream
- 2 cups strong brewed coffee, cooled
- 1/4 cup coffee liqueur (optional)
- 1 package ladyfingers (savoiardi)
- Cocoa powder for dusting

Instructions:

1. In a heatproof bowl, whisk together egg yolks and sugar until pale and creamy.
2. Place the bowl over a pot of simmering water, making sure the bottom of the bowl doesn't touch the water. Cook, stirring constantly, until the mixture thickens, about 5-7 minutes. Remove from heat and let cool slightly.
3. Add mascarpone cheese to the egg mixture and whisk until smooth.
4. In a separate bowl, whip the heavy cream until stiff peaks form. Gently fold the whipped cream into the mascarpone mixture until well combined.
5. Mix brewed coffee and coffee liqueur (if using) in a shallow dish.
6. Quickly dip each ladyfinger into the coffee mixture, making sure not to soak them too long.

7. Arrange a layer of dipped ladyfingers in the bottom of a serving dish.
8. Spread half of the mascarpone mixture over the ladyfingers.
9. Repeat with another layer of dipped ladyfingers and the remaining mascarpone mixture.
10. Cover and refrigerate for at least 4 hours, or overnight, to allow the flavors to meld.
11. Before serving, dust the top with cocoa powder. Slice and serve chilled.

B. Cannoli
Ingredients:

- 12 cannoli shells (store-bought or homemade)
- 1 1/2 cups ricotta cheese
- 1/2 cup powdered sugar
- 1/4 cup mini chocolate chips
- 1 teaspoon vanilla extract
- Candied fruit or chopped nuts for garnish (optional)

Instructions:

1. In a mixing bowl, combine ricotta cheese, powdered sugar, mini chocolate chips, and vanilla extract. Mix until well combined.
2. Spoon the ricotta mixture into a piping bag fitted with a large round tip.
3. Carefully pipe the ricotta mixture into each end of the cannoli shells, filling them completely.
4. Garnish the ends with candied fruit or chopped nuts if desired.
5. Serve immediately, or refrigerate until ready to serve. Cannoli are best enjoyed fresh.

C. Gelato
Ingredients:

- 2 cups whole milk
- 1 cup heavy cream
- 3/4 cup granulated sugar
- 4 egg yolks
- 1 teaspoon vanilla extract
- Flavors of your choice (such as chocolate, strawberry, or pistachio)

Instructions:

1. In a saucepan, heat whole milk and heavy cream over medium heat until it reaches a simmer. Remove from heat.
2. In a separate bowl, whisk together egg yolks and granulated sugar until pale and creamy.
3. Slowly pour the hot milk mixture into the egg mixture, whisking constantly to temper the eggs.
4. Pour the mixture back into the saucepan and cook over low heat, stirring constantly, until it thickens enough to coat the back of a spoon.
5. Remove from heat and stir in vanilla extract.
6. Strain the mixture through a fine-mesh sieve into a clean bowl to remove any lumps.
7. Cover and refrigerate until completely chilled, preferably overnight.
8. Churn the chilled mixture in an ice cream maker according to the manufacturer's instructions.
9. Transfer the churned gelato to a freezer-safe container and freeze for a few hours until firm.
10. Serve scoops of gelato in bowls or cones. Enjoy!

D. Affogato
Ingredients:

- 1 scoop vanilla gelato or ice cream per serving
- 1 shot (1-2 ounces) hot espresso per serving
- Optional: Amaretto, Frangelico, or other liqueurs for flavor variation

Instructions:

1. Place a scoop of vanilla gelato or ice cream in a serving glass or cup.
2. Pour a shot of hot espresso over the gelato.
3. Optionally, add a splash of liqueur for extra flavor.
4. Serve immediately with a spoon and enjoy the delightful combination of hot espresso and cold gelato melting together.

These desserts will perfectly complement your shrimp pasta dishes, offering a sweet and satisfying end to your meal. Enjoy!

Chapter (9) Quick and Easy Shrimp Pasta Recipes

A. One-Pot Garlic Butter Shrimp Pasta
Ingredients:

- 8 ounces linguine pasta
- 1/2 pound large shrimp, peeled and deveined
- 4 cloves garlic, minced
- 3 cups chicken broth (or vegetable broth)
- 1/4 cup unsalted butter
- 1/4 cup grated Parmesan cheese
- 2 tablespoons chopped fresh parsley
- Salt and pepper to taste
- Red pepper flakes for garnish (optional)

Instructions:

1. In a large pot or deep skillet, combine linguine pasta, minced garlic, chicken broth, and butter.
2. Bring the mixture to a boil over medium-high heat, then reduce the heat to medium-low and simmer uncovered, stirring occasionally, for about 10-12 minutes, or until the pasta is cooked and the liquid is mostly absorbed.
3. Add the peeled and deveined shrimp to the pot and cook for an additional 2-3 minutes, or until the shrimp are pink and opaque.
4. Stir in grated Parmesan cheese and chopped fresh parsley. Season with salt and pepper to taste.
5. Serve hot, garnished with red pepper flakes if desired. Enjoy your delicious one-pot garlic butter shrimp pasta!

B. Shrimp and Tomato Basil Pasta

Ingredients:

- 8 ounces spaghetti or penne pasta
- 1/2 pound large shrimp, peeled and deveined
- 2 tablespoons olive oil
- 4 cloves garlic, minced
- 1 can (14 ounces) diced tomatoes, drained
- 1/4 cup chopped fresh basil
- Salt and pepper to taste
- Grated Parmesan cheese for serving

Instructions:

1. Cook pasta according to package instructions until al dente. Drain and set aside.
2. In a large skillet, heat olive oil over medium heat. Add minced garlic and cook until fragrant, about 1 minute.
3. Add peeled and deveined shrimp to the skillet and cook until pink and opaque, about 2-3 minutes per side.
4. Stir in diced tomatoes and chopped fresh basil. Cook for another 2 minutes, allowing the flavors to meld.
5. Add cooked pasta to the skillet and toss everything together until well combined.
6. Season with salt and pepper to taste.
7. Serve hot, topped with grated Parmesan cheese. Enjoy your shrimp and tomato basil pasta!

C. Lemon Herb Shrimp Linguine
Ingredients:

- 8 ounces linguine pasta
- 1/2 pound large shrimp, peeled and deveined
- 2 tablespoons olive oil
- 2 cloves garlic, minced
- Zest and juice of 1 lemon
- 2 tablespoons chopped fresh parsley
- 1 tablespoon chopped fresh basil
- Salt and pepper to taste
- Grated Parmesan cheese for serving

Instructions:

1. Cook linguine pasta according to package instructions until al dente. Drain and set aside.
2. In a large skillet, heat olive oil over medium heat. Add minced garlic and cook until fragrant, about 1 minute.
3. Add peeled and deveined shrimp to the skillet and cook until pink and opaque, about 2-3 minutes per side.
4. Stir in lemon zest, lemon juice, chopped fresh parsley, and chopped fresh basil. Cook for another 2 minutes, allowing the flavors to meld.
5. Add cooked pasta to the skillet and toss everything together until well combined.
6. Season with salt and pepper to taste.
7. Serve hot, topped with grated Parmesan cheese. Enjoy your refreshing lemon herb shrimp linguine!

These quick and easy shrimp pasta recipes are perfect for busy weeknights when you want a delicious meal without spending hours in the kitchen. Enjoy!

Chapter (10) Shrimp Pasta for Special Occasions

A. Shrimp Scampi with Champagne Sauce
Ingredients:

- 8 ounces linguine pasta
- 1/2 pound large shrimp, peeled and deveined
- 4 tablespoons unsalted butter
- 4 cloves garlic, minced
- 1/4 cup chopped fresh parsley
- 1/2 cup champagne
- Zest and juice of 1 lemon
- Salt and pepper to taste
- Grated Parmesan cheese for serving
- Lemon slices and additional parsley for garnish

Instructions:

1. Cook linguine pasta according to package instructions until al dente. Drain and set aside.
2. In a large skillet, melt butter over medium heat. Add minced garlic and cook until fragrant, about 1 minute.
3. Add peeled and deveined shrimp to the skillet and cook until pink and opaque, about 2-3 minutes per side.
4. Stir in chopped fresh parsley, champagne, lemon zest, and lemon juice. Cook for another 2 minutes, allowing the flavors to meld and the sauce to slightly reduce.
5. Season with salt and pepper to taste.
6. Add cooked linguine pasta to the skillet and toss everything together until well combined.
7. Serve hot, garnished with grated Parmesan cheese, lemon slices,

and additional parsley. Enjoy your luxurious shrimp scampi with champagne sauce!

B. Lobster and Shrimp Ravioli with Creamy Tomato Sauce

Ingredients:

- 1 package (about 12 ounces) lobster and shrimp ravioli (store-bought or homemade)
- 2 tablespoons unsalted butter
- 2 cloves garlic, minced
- 1 cup heavy cream
- 1/2 cup grated Parmesan cheese
- 1/4 cup sun-dried tomatoes, chopped
- Salt and pepper to taste
- Fresh basil leaves for garnish

Instructions:

1. Cook lobster and shrimp ravioli according to package instructions until al dente. Drain and set aside.
2. In a large skillet, melt butter over medium heat. Add minced garlic and cook until fragrant, about 1 minute.
3. Pour in heavy cream and bring to a simmer. Cook for 2-3 minutes, stirring occasionally.
4. Stir in grated Parmesan cheese and chopped sun-dried tomatoes. Cook for another 2 minutes, until the sauce thickens slightly.
5. Season with salt and pepper to taste.
6. Add cooked lobster and shrimp ravioli to the skillet and toss gently to coat with the creamy tomato sauce.
7. Serve hot, garnished with fresh basil leaves. Enjoy your elegant lobster and shrimp ravioli with creamy tomato sauce!

C. Shrimp and Scallop Linguine with White Wine Sauce

Ingredients:

- 8 ounces linguine pasta
- 1/2 pound large shrimp, peeled and deveined
- 1/2 pound scallops, patted dry
- 4 tablespoons unsalted butter
- 4 cloves garlic, minced
- 1/2 cup dry white wine
- 1/2 cup heavy cream
- 2 tablespoons chopped fresh parsley
- Salt and pepper to taste
- Lemon wedges for serving

Instructions:

1. Cook linguine pasta according to package instructions until al dente. Drain and set aside.
2. In a large skillet, melt butter over medium heat. Add minced garlic and cook until fragrant, about 1 minute.
3. Add peeled and deveined shrimp to the skillet and cook until pink and opaque, about 2-3 minutes per side. Remove from skillet and set aside.
4. In the same skillet, add scallops and cook until golden brown on both sides, about 2-3 minutes per side. Remove from skillet and set aside.
5. Pour white wine into the skillet and bring to a simmer. Cook for 2-3 minutes, scraping up any browned bits from the bottom of the skillet.
6. Stir in heavy cream and chopped fresh parsley. Cook for another 2 minutes, until the sauce thickens slightly.
7. Season with salt and pepper to taste.
8. Add cooked linguine pasta, shrimp, and scallops to the skillet. Toss everything together until well coated in the white wine

sauce.

9. Serve hot, with lemon wedges on the side. Enjoy your indulgent shrimp and scallop linguine with white wine sauce!

These shrimp pasta dishes are perfect for special occasions, impressing your guests with their elegant flavors and luxurious presentation. Enjoy!

Chapter (11) Healthy Shrimp Pasta Options

A. Zucchini Noodles with Garlic Shrimp
   Ingredients:

- 2 medium zucchinis, spiralized into noodles
- 1/2 pound large shrimp, peeled and deveined
- 2 cloves garlic, minced
- 2 tablespoons olive oil
- 1 tablespoon lemon juice
- Salt and pepper to taste
- Chopped fresh parsley for garnish

Instructions:

1. Heat olive oil in a large skillet over medium heat. Add minced garlic and cook until fragrant, about 1 minute.
2. Add peeled and deveined shrimp to the skillet and cook until pink and opaque, about 2-3 minutes per side.
3. Add zucchini noodles to the skillet and toss with the shrimp and garlic.
4. Cook for 2-3 minutes, until the zucchini noodles are just tender but still crisp.
5. Remove from heat and drizzle with lemon juice. Season with salt and pepper to taste.
6. Serve hot, garnished with chopped fresh parsley.

B. Whole Wheat Spaghetti with Shrimp and Broccoli
   Ingredients:

- 8 ounces whole wheat spaghetti
- 1/2 pound large shrimp, peeled and deveined
- 2 cups broccoli florets
- 2 cloves garlic, minced
- 2 tablespoons olive oil
- 1 tablespoon lemon zest
- Salt and pepper to taste
- Grated Parmesan cheese for serving (optional)

Instructions:

1. Cook whole wheat spaghetti according to package instructions until al dente. Drain and set aside.
2. In a large pot of boiling water, blanch broccoli florets for 2-3 minutes, then drain and set aside.
3. Heat olive oil in a large skillet over medium heat. Add minced garlic and cook until fragrant, about 1 minute.
4. Add peeled and deveined shrimp to the skillet and cook until pink and opaque, about 2-3 minutes per side.
5. Add cooked whole wheat spaghetti and blanched broccoli florets to the skillet with the shrimp and garlic.
6. Toss everything together until well combined. Sprinkle with lemon zest and season with salt and pepper to taste.
7. Serve hot, with grated Parmesan cheese on top if desired.

C. Shrimp and Avocado Pasta Salad
Ingredients:

- 8 ounces whole grain pasta (such as penne or rotini)
- 1/2 pound large shrimp, peeled and deveined
- 1 avocado, diced
- 1 cup cherry tomatoes, halved
- 1/4 cup chopped red onion
- 2 tablespoons chopped fresh cilantro
- 2 tablespoons olive oil
- 1 tablespoon lime juice
- Salt and pepper to taste

Instructions:

1. Cook whole grain pasta according to package instructions until al dente. Drain and set aside.
2. In a large pot of boiling water, blanch shrimp for 2-3 minutes, then drain and set aside.
3. In a large bowl, combine cooked pasta, blanched shrimp, diced avocado, cherry tomatoes, chopped red onion, and chopped fresh cilantro.
4. In a small bowl, whisk together olive oil and lime juice. Pour over the pasta salad and toss until everything is well coated.
5. Season with salt and pepper to taste.
6. Serve chilled or at room temperature.

These healthy shrimp pasta options are packed with flavor and nutrients, making them perfect for a satisfying and nutritious meal. Enjoy!

Chapter (12) Seasonal Shrimp Pasta Dishes

A. Summer Shrimp Pasta with Fresh Basil and Tomatoes

Ingredients:

- 8 ounces spaghetti or linguine pasta
- 1/2 pound large shrimp, peeled and deveined
- 2 tablespoons olive oil
- 3 cloves garlic, minced
- 2 cups cherry tomatoes, halved
- 1/4 cup chopped fresh basil leaves
- Zest and juice of 1 lemon
- Salt and pepper to taste
- Grated Parmesan cheese for serving (optional)

Instructions:

1. Cook pasta according to package instructions until al dente. Drain and set aside.
2. In a large skillet, heat olive oil over medium heat. Add minced garlic and cook until fragrant, about 1 minute.
3. Add peeled and deveined shrimp to the skillet and cook until pink and opaque, about 2-3 minutes per side.
4. Add cherry tomatoes to the skillet and cook for another 2-3 minutes, until they start to soften and release their juices.
5. Stir in chopped fresh basil, lemon zest, and lemon juice. Cook for another minute to allow the flavors to meld.
6. Add cooked pasta to the skillet and toss everything together until well combined.
7. Season with salt and pepper to taste.
8. Serve hot, with grated Parmesan cheese on top if desired. Enjoy

your light and refreshing summer shrimp pasta!

B. Fall Harvest Shrimp and Butternut Squash Pasta
Ingredients:

- 8 ounces penne or fusilli pasta
- 1/2 pound large shrimp, peeled and deveined
- 2 cups butternut squash, peeled and diced
- 2 tablespoons olive oil
- 2 cloves garlic, minced
- 1/4 teaspoon ground cinnamon
- 1/4 teaspoon ground nutmeg
- Salt and pepper to taste
- 1/4 cup chopped fresh sage leaves
- Grated Parmesan cheese for serving

Instructions:

1. Cook pasta according to package instructions until al dente. Drain and set aside.
2. In a large skillet, heat olive oil over medium heat. Add minced garlic and cook until fragrant, about 1 minute.
3. Add diced butternut squash to the skillet and cook until tender, about 8-10 minutes, stirring occasionally.
4. Push the butternut squash to one side of the skillet and add peeled and deveined shrimp to the other side. Cook shrimp until pink and opaque, about 2-3 minutes per side.
5. Sprinkle ground cinnamon and ground nutmeg over the butternut squash and shrimp. Season with salt and pepper to taste.
6. Add cooked pasta to the skillet and toss everything together until well combined.
7. Stir in chopped fresh sage leaves.

8. Serve hot, with grated Parmesan cheese on top. Enjoy your cozy fall harvest shrimp and butternut squash pasta!

C. Winter Comfort: Shrimp and Creamy Parmesan Polenta
Ingredients:

- 1 cup cornmeal
- 4 cups water
- 1/2 cup grated Parmesan cheese
- Salt and pepper to taste
- 1/2 pound large shrimp, peeled and deveined
- 2 tablespoons olive oil
- 2 cloves garlic, minced
- 2 cups baby spinach leaves
- Red pepper flakes for garnish (optional)

Instructions:

1. In a medium saucepan, bring water to a boil. Slowly whisk in cornmeal, stirring constantly to prevent lumps.
2. Reduce heat to low and cook, stirring occasionally, until the polenta is thick and creamy, about 15-20 minutes.
3. Stir in grated Parmesan cheese and season with salt and pepper to taste. Keep warm.
4. In a large skillet, heat olive oil over medium heat. Add minced garlic and cook until fragrant, about 1 minute.
5. Add peeled and deveined shrimp to the skillet and cook until pink and opaque, about 2-3 minutes per side.
6. Add baby spinach leaves to the skillet and cook until wilted, about 1-2 minutes.
7. Serve creamy Parmesan polenta topped with garlic shrimp and spinach.
8. Garnish with red pepper flakes if desired. Enjoy your

comforting winter shrimp and creamy Parmesan polenta dish!

These seasonal shrimp pasta dishes are perfect for enjoying the flavors of each season and making the most of fresh, seasonal ingredients. Enjoy!

Chapter (13) Shrimp Pasta Around the World: Regional Specialties

A. Japanese Shrimp Udon Noodles
Ingredients:

- 8 ounces udon noodles
- 1/2 pound large shrimp, peeled and deveined
- 2 cups dashi broth
- 2 tablespoons soy sauce
- 1 tablespoon mirin
- 1 tablespoon sake (optional)
- 1 tablespoon sesame oil
- 1 cup sliced shiitake mushrooms
- 2 green onions, sliced
- Nori (seaweed) strips for garnish (optional)
- Shichimi togarashi (Japanese seven spice blend) for garnish (optional)

Instructions:

1. Cook udon noodles according to package instructions until al dente. Drain and set aside.
2. In a large pot, bring dashi broth to a simmer over medium heat.
3. Add soy sauce, mirin, and sake (if using) to the pot. Stir to combine.
4. Add peeled and deveined shrimp, sliced shiitake mushrooms, and sliced green onions to the pot. Cook until the shrimp are pink and opaque, about 2-3 minutes.
5. Add cooked udon noodles to the pot and toss everything together until well combined.
6. Drizzle sesame oil over the udon noodles and shrimp mixture.

Stir to incorporate.

7. Serve hot, garnished with nori strips and shichimi togarashi if desired. Enjoy your delicious Japanese shrimp udon noodles!

B. Indian Shrimp Curry Pasta
Ingredients:

- 8 ounces penne pasta
- 1/2 pound large shrimp, peeled and deveined
- 2 tablespoons vegetable oil
- 1 onion, finely chopped
- 2 cloves garlic, minced
- 1 tablespoon grated ginger
- 2 tomatoes, chopped
- 1 tablespoon curry powder
- 1 teaspoon ground turmeric
- 1 teaspoon ground cumin
- 1/2 teaspoon ground coriander
- 1/4 teaspoon cayenne pepper (optional)
- 1 cup coconut milk
- Salt and pepper to taste
- Chopped fresh cilantro for garnish

Instructions:

1. Cook penne pasta according to package instructions until al dente. Drain and set aside.
2. In a large skillet, heat vegetable oil over medium heat. Add finely chopped onion and cook until softened, about 5 minutes.
3. Add minced garlic and grated ginger to the skillet. Cook for another 1-2 minutes until fragrant.
4. Stir in chopped tomatoes, curry powder, ground turmeric, ground cumin, ground coriander, and cayenne pepper (if

using). Cook until the tomatoes break down and the spices are fragrant, about 5-7 minutes.

5. Add peeled and deveined shrimp to the skillet and cook until pink and opaque, about 2-3 minutes.
6. Pour in coconut milk and stir to combine. Simmer for 5 minutes to allow the flavors to meld and the sauce to thicken slightly.
7. Season with salt and pepper to taste.
8. Add cooked penne pasta to the skillet and toss everything together until well coated.
9. Serve hot, garnished with chopped fresh cilantro. Enjoy your flavorful Indian shrimp curry pasta!

C. Greek Shrimp Orzo Salad
Ingredients:

- 8 ounces orzo pasta
- 1/2 pound large shrimp, peeled and deveined
- 2 tablespoons olive oil
- 2 cloves garlic, minced
- 1 cup cherry tomatoes, halved
- 1/2 cup cucumber, diced
- 1/4 cup Kalamata olives, pitted and sliced
- 1/4 cup crumbled feta cheese
- 2 tablespoons chopped fresh dill
- 1 tablespoon lemon juice
- Salt and pepper to taste

Instructions:

1. Cook orzo pasta according to package instructions until al dente. Drain and set aside.
2. In a large skillet, heat olive oil over medium heat. Add minced

garlic and cook until fragrant, about 1 minute.

3. Add peeled and deveined shrimp to the skillet and cook until pink and opaque, about 2-3 minutes per side.
4. In a large mixing bowl, combine cooked orzo pasta, cooked shrimp, halved cherry tomatoes, diced cucumber, sliced Kalamata olives, crumbled feta cheese, chopped fresh dill, and lemon juice.
5. Toss everything together until well combined.
6. Season with salt and pepper to taste.
7. Serve chilled or at room temperature. Enjoy your refreshing Greek shrimp orzo salad!

These shrimp pasta dishes showcase the diverse flavors and ingredients from around the world, providing a delicious culinary journey for your taste buds. Enjoy!

Chapter (14) Cooking Techniques: Perfecting Shrimp Preparation

A. How to Peel and Devein Shrimp

Peeling and deveining shrimp is an essential step in preparing them for cooking. Here's a simple guide to help you:

Ingredients/Tools:

- Fresh shrimp
- Cutting board
- Paring knife or shrimp deveiner
- Bowl of cold water

Instructions:

- Start by rinsing the shrimp under cold water to remove any dirt or debris.
- Lay the shrimp flat on a cutting board.
- To peel the shrimp, hold the body with one hand and gently grip the shell with your other hand. Peel the shell off starting from the legs and working your way towards the tail. You can leave the tail intact for presentation if desired.

To devein the shrimp, you have two options:

- Use a paring knife: Make a shallow incision along the back of the shrimp where the vein is located. Use the tip of the knife to lift out the vein and discard it.
- Use a shrimp deveiner: Insert the pointed end of the deveiner tool under the vein along the back of the shrimp. Gently pull the tool upwards to lift out the vein.
- Once peeled and deveined, rinse the shrimp again under cold water to remove any remaining debris.

- Pat the shrimp dry with paper towels before using them in your recipe.

B. Marinating Shrimp for Maximum Flavor

Marinating shrimp is a great way to infuse them with flavor before cooking. Here's how to do it:

Ingredients/Tools:

- Fresh shrimp
- Marinade of your choice (e.g., garlic, lemon, herbs, soy sauce, etc.)
- Bowl or resealable plastic bag

Instructions:

1. Prepare the marinade by combining your desired ingredients in a bowl. You can use a combination of garlic, lemon juice, herbs, soy sauce, olive oil, and spices to create your marinade.
2. Add the shrimp to the marinade, making sure they are evenly coated. You can marinate the shrimp in a bowl or transfer them to a resealable plastic bag for easier storage and distribution of the marinade.
3. Seal the bowl or bag and refrigerate for at least 30 minutes, or up to 2 hours, to allow the shrimp to soak up the flavors.
4. If using wooden skewers for grilling, soak them in water for about 30 minutes before threading the shrimp onto them to prevent burning.
5. After marinating, remove the shrimp from the marinade and discard any excess marinade.
6. Cook the shrimp according to your preferred method, such as grilling, sautéing, or baking.

C. Grilling vs. Sauteing: Choosing the Right Cooking Method

Both grilling and sautéing are excellent methods for cooking shrimp, but they offer slightly different flavors and textures. Here's a comparison to help you choose the right method for your dish:

Grilling:

- Grilling shrimp over an open flame imparts a smoky flavor and creates beautiful grill marks.
- Preheat your grill to medium-high heat and lightly oil the grates to prevent sticking.
- Thread marinated shrimp onto skewers for easy flipping.
- Grill shrimp for 2-3 minutes per side, or until they are pink and opaque.
- Grilled shrimp are perfect for serving as a main dish, appetizer, or as part of a skewer with vegetables.

Sautéing:

- Sautéing shrimp in a skillet on the stovetop allows for quick cooking and easy flavor customization.
- Heat a skillet over medium-high heat and add a small amount of oil or butter.
- Add seasoned shrimp to the skillet in a single layer, making sure not to overcrowd the pan.
- Sauté shrimp for 2-3 minutes per side, or until they are pink and opaque.
- Sautéed shrimp are versatile and can be used in a variety of dishes, such as pasta, stir-fries, salads, and tacos.

Choose the cooking method that best suits your preferences and the flavor profile of your dish. Whether you opt for the smoky char of grilled shrimp or the quick sear of sautéed shrimp, you're sure to enjoy delicious results!

Chapter (15) Pasta Pairings: Finding the Right Pasta for Your Shrimp Dish

A. Matching Pasta Shapes with Sauce Consistencies

Choosing the right pasta shape for your shrimp dish can significantly enhance the overall dining experience. Here's a guide to help you pair pasta shapes with sauce consistencies:

Long and Thin Pasta (e.g., Linguine, Spaghetti):

- Best paired with light and delicate sauces such as olive oil-based sauces, garlic butter sauces, and simple tomato sauces.
- Ideal for shrimp scampi, shrimp aglio e olio, and shrimp marinara.

Flat Ribbon Pasta (e.g., Fettuccine, Tagliatelle):

- Perfect for rich and creamy sauces like Alfredo sauce or cheese-based sauces.
- Ideal for creamy garlic shrimp fettuccine Alfredo and shrimp carbonara.

Short and Tubular Pasta (e.g., Penne, Rigatoni):

- Excellent for holding chunky sauces and ingredients, making them suitable for hearty shrimp pasta dishes.
- Ideal for spicy shrimp arrabbiata penne and shrimp and sausage pasta.

Shaped Pasta (e.g., Farfalle, Rotini, Shells):

- Versatile and can be paired with a variety of sauces, including creamy sauces, tomato-based sauces, and pesto.
- Ideal for shrimp and pesto farfalle, shrimp and spinach stuffed

shells, and shrimp macaroni salad.

B. Gluten-Free Pasta Options for Shrimp Lovers

For those following a gluten-free diet, there are plenty of pasta alternatives available that pair well with shrimp dishes. Here are some **popular gluten-free pasta options:**

1. Brown Rice Pasta: Made from brown rice flour, this pasta has a slightly nutty flavor and a texture similar to traditional pasta. It works well with most shrimp sauces.
2. Quinoa Pasta: Quinoa pasta is made from quinoa flour and has a light, fluffy texture. It pairs nicely with shrimp and vegetable stir-fries or light garlic sauces.
3. Corn Pasta: Corn pasta is made from corn flour and has a slightly sweet taste. It's sturdy enough to hold up to creamy sauces, making it a good choice for shrimp Alfredo dishes.
4. Chickpea Pasta: Made from chickpea flour, this pasta has a slightly nutty flavor and is high in protein and fiber. It pairs well with spicy shrimp arrabbiata or shrimp curry dishes.
5. Zucchini Noodles (Zoodles): For a low-carb, gluten-free option, consider using zucchini noodles as a base for your shrimp pasta dishes. They work well with light sauces and are packed with nutrients.

C. Homemade Pasta vs. Store-Bought: Pros and Cons

When it comes to choosing between homemade and store-bought pasta for your shrimp dishes, there are advantages and disadvantages to consider:

Homemade Pasta:

Pros:

- Fresh flavor and texture.

- Can be customized with different ingredients such as whole wheat flour or herbs.
- Satisfaction of making pasta from scratch.

Cons:

- Time-consuming process, especially if making large quantities.
- Requires special equipment like a pasta machine or rolling pin.
- May not have the same consistency as store-bought pasta, especially for beginners.

Store-Bought Pasta:
Pros:

- Convenient and time-saving, as it's ready to cook.
- Wide variety of shapes and types available.
- Consistent texture and cooking time.

Cons:

- May contain preservatives or additives.
- Limited customization options compared to homemade pasta.
- Quality may vary depending on the brand and type.

Ultimately, the choice between homemade and store-bought pasta depends on your personal preferences, time constraints, and willingness to experiment in the kitchen. Both options can yield delicious shrimp pasta dishes when paired with the right sauces and ingredients.

Chapter (16) Wine and Beverage Pairings with Shrimp Pasta

A. White Wine Recommendations for Shrimp Pasta

White wine is a classic pairing for shrimp pasta dishes, as its crisp acidity and fruity notes complement the delicate flavors of the seafood. Here are some white wine recommendations to enhance your shrimp pasta experience:

1. Pinot Grigio: With its light, refreshing character and citrusy notes, Pinot Grigio pairs well with a variety of shrimp pasta dishes, especially those with garlic and lemon flavors.
2. Chardonnay: Chardonnay offers a richer and creamier profile, making it a great match for creamy shrimp pasta dishes like fettuccine Alfredo or shrimp risotto.
3. Sauvignon Blanc: Known for its zesty acidity and herbaceous aromas, Sauvignon Blanc pairs beautifully with shrimp dishes featuring fresh herbs, green vegetables, or tangy sauces.
4. Vermentino: This Mediterranean white wine offers crisp acidity and vibrant fruit flavors, making it an excellent choice for pairing with shrimp scampi or seafood pasta salads.
5. Gewürztraminer: With its aromatic profile of lychee, rose petals, and spice, Gewürztraminer adds complexity to shrimp pasta dishes with Asian-inspired flavors or fruity sauces.

B. Beer Pairings for Spicy Shrimp Dishes

For spicy shrimp pasta dishes, beer can be a refreshing and palate-cleansing beverage choice. Here are some beer styles that complement the heat and flavors of spicy shrimp dishes:

1. Wheat Beer: The crisp, refreshing character of wheat beer pairs well with spicy shrimp pasta dishes, balancing the heat with its

smooth and slightly sweet profile.

2. India Pale Ale (IPA): The hoppy bitterness of an IPA can cut through the spiciness of shrimp dishes, while its citrusy and piney notes complement the bold flavors of the dish.

3. Saison: With its effervescence and complex flavors of spice, fruit, and yeast, saison adds depth to spicy shrimp pasta dishes without overpowering them.

4. Belgian Tripel: This strong and fruity ale offers sweetness and complexity, which can complement the heat of spicy shrimp pasta dishes while providing a refreshing contrast.

5. Mexican Lager: Light and crisp, Mexican lager provides a clean palate to reset between bites of spicy shrimp pasta, while its subtle maltiness enhances the flavors of the dish.

C. Non-Alcoholic Alternatives: Mocktails and Refreshing Beverages

For those who prefer non-alcoholic options or want to offer alternatives to guests, here are some refreshing mocktails and beverages to enjoy with shrimp pasta:

1. Citrus Sparkler: Mix sparkling water with freshly squeezed lemon or lime juice, a splash of simple syrup, and a few sprigs of mint for a refreshing and tangy mocktail.

2. Iced Herbal Tea: Brew a batch of herbal tea, such as mint, chamomile, or hibiscus, and chill it in the refrigerator. Serve over ice with a squeeze of lemon for a cooling beverage option.

3. Cucumber Mint Cooler: Blend cucumber slices with fresh mint leaves, lime juice, and a touch of honey. Strain the mixture and serve over ice for a revitalizing and hydrating drink.

4. Ginger Beer Spritz: Mix ginger beer with a splash of sparkling water and a squeeze of lemon or lime. Garnish with a slice of citrus or a sprig of mint for a zesty and effervescent beverage.

5. Virgin Mojito: Muddle fresh mint leaves with lime wedges and

a spoonful of sugar in a glass. Fill the glass with crushed ice and top with soda water for a refreshing and minty mocktail.

These wine and beverage pairings will enhance the flavors of your shrimp pasta dishes and provide a delightful accompaniment to your meal, whether you prefer white wine, beer, or non-alcoholic beverages. Cheers to a fantastic dining experience!

Chapter (17) Shrimp Pasta for Kids and Picky Eaters

A. Shrimp Mac and Cheese

Ingredients:

- 8 ounces elbow macaroni
- 1/2 pound small shrimp, peeled and deveined
- 2 tablespoons butter
- 2 tablespoons all-purpose flour
- 2 cups milk
- 2 cups shredded cheddar cheese
- Salt and pepper to taste
- Optional: breadcrumbs for topping

Instructions:

1. Cook the elbow macaroni according to package instructions until al dente. Drain and set aside.
2. In a large skillet, melt the butter over medium heat. Add the flour and cook, stirring constantly, for about 1 minute to make a roux.
3. Gradually whisk in the milk, stirring constantly to avoid lumps. Cook until the mixture thickens, about 5 minutes.
4. Reduce the heat to low and add the shredded cheddar cheese to the skillet. Stir until the cheese is melted and the sauce is smooth.
5. Add the cooked macaroni and shrimp to the cheese sauce, stirring until well combined. Season with salt and pepper to taste.
6. Optional: Transfer the shrimp mac and cheese to a baking dish, sprinkle breadcrumbs over the top, and broil for a few minutes

until golden brown and bubbly.

7. Serve hot and enjoy this kid-friendly twist on a classic comfort food favorite!

B. Hidden Veggie Shrimp Spaghetti
Ingredients:

- 8 ounces spaghetti
- 1/2 pound small shrimp, peeled and deveined
- 1 tablespoon olive oil
- 2 cloves garlic, minced
- 1 cup tomato sauce
- 1/2 cup finely chopped vegetables (e.g., carrots, zucchini, bell peppers)
- Salt and pepper to taste
- Grated Parmesan cheese for serving

Instructions:

1. Cook the spaghetti according to package instructions until al dente. Drain and set aside.
2. In a large skillet, heat the olive oil over medium heat. Add the minced garlic and cook until fragrant, about 1 minute.
3. Add the finely chopped vegetables to the skillet and cook until they start to soften, about 5 minutes.
4. Stir in the tomato sauce and bring the mixture to a simmer.
5. Add the shrimp to the skillet and cook until they are pink and opaque, about 2-3 minutes per side.
6. Add the cooked spaghetti to the skillet and toss everything together until well coated. Season with salt and pepper to taste.
7. Serve hot, garnished with grated Parmesan cheese. Kids will love this delicious spaghetti packed with hidden veggies and shrimp!

C. Mini Shrimp Alfredo Pizzas
   Ingredients:

- Mini pizza crusts or English muffins
- 1/2 cup Alfredo sauce
- 1/2 pound small shrimp, peeled and deveined
- 1 cup shredded mozzarella cheese
- Optional toppings: sliced tomatoes, chopped spinach, sliced mushrooms

Instructions:

1. Preheat your oven to 400°F (200°C).
2. Place mini pizza crusts or halved English muffins on a baking sheet.
3. Spread Alfredo sauce evenly over each pizza crust or English muffin half.
4. Top with cooked shrimp and any optional toppings of your choice.
5. Sprinkle shredded mozzarella cheese over the toppings.
6. Bake in the preheated oven for 10-12 minutes, or until the cheese is melted and bubbly.
7. Allow the mini shrimp Alfredo pizzas to cool slightly before serving. Enjoy these fun and tasty pizzas that are sure to be a hit with kids and picky eaters alike!

These shrimp pasta recipes offer kid-friendly twists and creative ways to incorporate seafood into meals for even the pickiest eaters. Enjoy making and sharing these delicious dishes with your family!

Chapter (18) Shrimp Pasta Garnishes and Toppings

A. Fresh Herbs: Parsley, Basil, and Chives

Fresh herbs can elevate the flavor and presentation of shrimp pasta dishes. Here's how to use them as garnishes:

- Parsley: Finely chop fresh parsley leaves and sprinkle them over the finished dish. Parsley adds a fresh, slightly peppery flavor and vibrant green color to shrimp pasta.
- Basil: Tear or chiffonade fresh basil leaves and scatter them on top of the pasta. Basil lends a sweet, aromatic flavor that pairs beautifully with shrimp and tomato-based sauces.
- Chives: Slice fresh chives into small pieces and sprinkle them over the pasta for a subtle onion flavor and a pop of color. Chives complement the delicate taste of shrimp and add visual appeal to the dish.

B. Citrus Zest: Lemon, Lime, and Orange

Citrus zest adds brightness and acidity to shrimp pasta dishes. Here's how to incorporate it as a topping:

- Lemon Zest: Use a fine grater or zester to remove the outer yellow zest from a lemon. Sprinkle the lemon zest over the pasta just before serving to impart a refreshing citrus aroma and tangy flavor.
- Lime Zest: Follow the same process with a lime to obtain fragrant lime zest. Lime zest adds a zesty kick and tropical flair to shrimp pasta, especially dishes with Asian or Caribbean-inspired flavors.
- Orange Zest: Grate the outer orange zest from an orange and sprinkle it over the pasta for a citrusy twist. Orange zest adds a

hint of sweetness and complexity to shrimp pasta, particularly dishes with creamy sauces.

C. Toasted Bread Crumbs and Pine Nuts

Toasted bread crumbs and pine nuts add texture and depth to shrimp pasta dishes. Here's how to prepare and use them as toppings:

- Toasted Bread Crumbs: Heat a skillet over medium heat and add plain bread crumbs. Cook, stirring frequently, until the bread crumbs turn golden brown and crisp. Sprinkle the toasted bread crumbs over the pasta to add a crunchy contrast to the tender shrimp and pasta.

- Toasted Pine Nuts: In the same skillet, toast pine nuts over medium heat until they become golden brown and fragrant, shaking the pan frequently to prevent burning. Sprinkle the toasted pine nuts over the pasta for a nutty crunch and rich flavor that complements the shrimp.

These garnishes and toppings offer a variety of flavors and textures to enhance your shrimp pasta dishes. Experiment with different combinations to create visually stunning and delicious meals that will impress your guests!

❖ Conclusion

A. Final Thoughts on Shrimp Pasta Mastery

Mastering the art of shrimp pasta opens up a world of culinary possibilities, where the delicate flavors of seafood intertwine with the comforting embrace of pasta. From classic recipes to innovative creations, shrimp pasta offers endless opportunities for creativity and exploration in the kitchen. Remember to savor each bite, appreciate the quality of ingredients, and embrace the joy of cooking as you embark on your shrimp pasta journey.

B. Invitation to Continue Exploring Shrimp Pasta Creations

As you conclude your exploration of shrimp pasta, we invite you to continue your culinary journey by exploring new recipes, techniques, and flavor combinations. Whether you're drawn to traditional Italian dishes, international flavors, or inventive twists on familiar favorites, there's always something new to discover in the world of shrimp pasta. Let your creativity soar, and don't hesitate to share your delicious creations with friends and family.

C. Bon Appétit!

With that, we bid you farewell and wish you many delightful moments of culinary delight with your shrimp pasta creations. May each dish bring joy to your table and satisfaction to your palate. Bon appétit!

www.ingramcontent.com/pod-product-compliance
Lightning Source LLC
Chambersburg PA
CBHW051817130726
47987CB00003B/1300

* 9 7 9 8 2 2 4 0 1 3 4 1 8 *